DOG TRAINING INSIGHTS

*Conversations With America's
Leading Dog Trainers*

DOG TRAINING INSIGHTS
Conversations With America's Leading Dog Trainers

Featuring:

Neil Cohen

Curtis Day

Tom Longenecker

Audra Mather

HP Parvizian

Lisa York

Royalties from the retail sales of **"DOG TRAINING INSIGHTS: CONVERSATIONS WITH AMERICA'S LEADING DOG TRAINERS"** are donated to the Global Autism Project:

AUTISM KNOWS NO BORDERS;
FORTUNATELY NEITHER DO WE.®

The Global Autism Project 501(C)3, is a nonprofit organization which provides training to local individuals in evidence-based practice for individuals with autism.

The Global Autism Project believes that every child has the ability to learn and their potential should not be limited by geographical bounds.

The Global Autism Project seeks to eliminate the disparity in service provision seen around the world by providing high-quality training to individuals providing services in their local community. This training is made sustainable through regular training trips and contiguous remote training.

You can learn more about the Global Autism Project by visiting **GlobalAutismProject.org**

Dog Training Insights / America's Leading Dog Trainers —1st ed.

Managing Editor/ Shannon Buritz

ISBN-13: 978-1-7323763-6-6

TABLE OF CONTENTS

A NOTE TO THE READER

Thank you for buying your copy of "DOG TRAINING INSIGHTS: Conversations With America's Leading Dog Trainers." This book was originally created as a series of live interviews, that's why it reads like a series of conversations, rather than a traditional book that talks at you.

I wanted you to feel as though the participants and I are talking with you, much like a close friend, or relative, and felt that creating the material this way would make it easier for you to grasp the topics and put them to use quickly, rather than wading through hundreds of pages.

So relax, grab a pen and paper, take notes and get ready to learn some fascinating Dog Training Insights.

Warmest regards,

Mark Imperial
Publisher, Author and Radio Personality

INTRODUCTION

"**DOG TRAINING INSIGHTS: Conversations With America's Leading Dog Trainers**" is a collaborative book series featuring leading dog trainers from across the country who are passionate about helping you and your pet. Get valuable advice from this round table discussion with an elite panel of experts representing Sit Means Sit Dog Training: Neil Cohen (New York), Curtis Day (Wyoming), Tom Longenecker (New York), Audra Mather (Michigan), HP Parvizian (Texas), and Lisa York (Texas).

Remarkable Press™ would like to extend a heartfelt thank you to all participants who took the time to submit their chapter and offer their support in becoming ambassadors for this project.

100% of the royalties from the retail sales of this book will be donated to the Global Autism Project. Should you want to make a direct donation, visit their website at: GlobalAutismProject.org

ABOUT "SIT MEANS SIT"

Sit Means Sit, founded by Fred Hassen, offers an evolutionary dog training system – a studied, tested, proven, specialized approach that shows immediate results in the dog's ability to maintain focus to the task at hand even around distractions in a non-confrontational way. These methods have earned Fred the opportunity to train not only the general dog owner's dog, but dogs owned by celebrities and professional athletes from around the globe as well.

Sit Means Sit trainers all go through intensive, proprietary training for 21 days when they begin their franchise and then 80-100 hours a year of continuing education. Additionally, every certified trainer must recertify every three years to maintain their status and keep current on our training system.

Sit Means Sit currently has over 140 locations in the US and Canada, training over 1800 dogs per month. Sit Means Sit dogs have competed and won in every dog sport, have been featured on national and local TV and we proudly have the largest therapy dog team in the country, with over 900 handler teams.

For more information about opening your own Sit Means Sit franchise, please visit us at
https://sitmeanssit.com/franchise/

Dog Training Myths and Misconceptions

Neil Cohen: A big misconception exists regarding the element of "fear" in dog training. Many people believe that if your dog doesn't fear you, he is not going to listen to you. They assume that training must have more to it than giving out rewards and cookies, and that the missing piece has to be fear. Like anything else in life, we need balance in our training. It is important to develop an understanding of consequences. The word "consequence" often has a negative connotation associated with it. In reality, consequences are neutral. For example, if you get an "A" on a test and your mom gives you a hug, praise, hangs it on the refrigerator and gives you a cookie, those are all consequences of your hard work. So consequences are simply "if you do A, then B happens."

Secondly, I see many people who are in constant conflict with their dog when attempting to train. For example, when teaching a dog to sit, I often hear from owners say "SIT" while waiving a cookie in front of me. But my "trainer's brain" hears "you will sit calmly or I will NOT give you a cookie." which ultimately creates a lot of unnecessary tension and conflict. We really need to focus on aligning what we are trying to do, and celebrating each accomplishment of the dog.

Lastly, a misconception exists that obedience is defined by tricks. Obedience is not tricks. Having your dog sit on command is a trick. Your dog knows how to put his behind on the ground, and getting him to do that when you tell him to is doing a trick on command. Obedience is the ability to follow commands and be able to do those tricks, with distractions present. A dog with a high level of obedience for sitting will do the trick even with seventeen dancing squirrels juggling cheeseburgers right in front of him. We want to move the dog along that trajectory, building up his reliability to follow commands and perform the trick in any situation. This is true obedience.

Curtis Day: A common misconception is that choke chains or pinch collars are effective training tools. Unfortunately, these tools are often used incorrectly. I incorporate the use of E-collars into my training. With 100% of the training I perform, the main focus is getting the dog's attention on the trainer/owner so we can teach and reward good behavior. The way I use the E-collar is essentially a "tap on the shoulder" for the dog in order to get that attention. I do not believe in punishment or extreme correction through the use of choke chains or pinch collars.

Tom Longenecker: The number one misconception is that dog training is only for "bad" or "aggressive" dogs. The first thing people often say to me is "My dog is a good dog." Obedience training is for ALL dogs. Instead of spending your valuable time trying to navigate the training process on your own, working with a professional allows you to "help you help your dog". Whether you are trying to get your dog to walk nicely on a leash, dealing with aggression issues, or just trying to set a new puppy on the path to success, a dog trainer can help you get more out of life with your dog.

Audra Mather: A myth that is perpetuated in our industry is that spaying/neutering will fix your dog's behavior issues. I believe this myth began way back in the day when we didn't have fences or leashes for our dogs. Dogs were just left to wander. So if there was a female dog down the road that was causing your male dog to constantly cross the street to visit her, neutering would SEEM to be a solution to correct this behavior. It would make the visits less frequent and prevent your dog from dangerously crossing the street. As time went by, narratives like this made people believe that altering dogs could actually change behavior. In reality, spaying/neutering is a personal decision and has no bearing on behavior modification. No matter what decision you make for your dog, just make sure that you strive to be a responsible dog owner.

Secondly, people believe that an older dog in the household will "train your puppy" for you. A puppy will certainly "mimic" the behaviors of an older dog. But what if that dog is not as well trained as you would like? What if he barks at people, dashes out the front door every chance he gets, and wildly jumps on guests entering your home? You will soon find that the puppy is engaging in these behaviors as well. Therefore, it is better to leave training to the humans.

Lastly, no two dogs are the same. There is no "one size fits all" training program. Even with two dogs of the same breed, you may see two completely different personality types. For example, let's say you have two Golden Retrievers. One might be "happy go lucky". The sun is shining, the day is long..let's go frolic! On the other hand, we have a second dog who is fearful of the neighbors and the garbage man. He barks frantically and displays leash reactivity. These two dogs will need to be treated very differently. The "happy go lucky" dog probably needs a bit of impulse control to harness some of that exuberant energy. The fearful dog needs a training program designed to build confidence. The needs of the owners could be very different as well. One owner could be very busy with a spouse and children. Another owner could be single and able to devote all of their time to the dog. I create programs to cater to the needs of the specific owners so they can easily incorporate training into their unique lifestyle. Anybody can have a well trained dog!

HP Parvizian: I find that many people make training more difficult than it really is. Dog training does not require a lot of work or a lot of commands. And the few commands that we do use have very simple meanings. There is no need to over complicate a command. For example, if I tell my dog to "come", it means I want him within petting distance. That's it. This command tells my dog to come to me, keep his head within petting distance, and pay attention. If my dog is across the room, he knows he will need to move toward me to achieve the desired results.

Another example illustrating the importance of defining commands is the game of "fetch". I often hear people say "My dog will go get the item, but he won't bring it back to me." In this scenario, we have to be careful about our definition of the command "fetch." When I play this game with my dogs, "fetch" simply means "put the object in your mouth." Once the dog has the object in his mouth, the next command is "come." Once the dog comes, I have him "sit". Lastly, I ask the dog to drop the item by commanding "out." These are four simple commands that are very clearly defined, taking the guesswork out of what the game should look like.

By simplifying training, we take the stress out of it. We break it down all the way to the basic level of simple, easy to follow commands. Instead of trying to force our dogs to do what we want, we simply need to redirect focus to the desired task. Training should be fun and occur naturally during the time you spend with your dog.

Lisa York: A common myth exists around the concept of potty training and effective correction. Many people think that rubbing the dogs' nose in the accident and scolding them is the best form of correction, which is simply not true and does nothing to achieve the desired behavior.

Another myth is that certain dogs CANNOT be trained. We hear all the time "My dog is one year old. Is it too late to train him?" The simple answer is that it is NEVER too late. I can train a 12 year old dog. And though some factors may vary (he may not sit as quickly as a younger dog), the fact remains that a dog's brain never stops working due to age. Whether young or old, all dogs are trainable.

If you would like more information or to find a "Sit Means Sit" near you, please visit www.sitmeanssit.com

How Do I Get My Dog to Stop Jumping?

Neil Cohen: So the first thing that I would say is that I've got a problem with the question. Not that it's a bad question, but we have to consider basic behavioral definitions, the question is only focusing on eliminating a behavior. Behaviorists would say we need to focus on more than just eliminating because there are actually two parts to the equation. Behaviors that we want to see less of should be corrected. But we cannot forget to reward and reinforce the behaviors we want to see MORE of. I like to shift the focus to behaviors we WANT the dog to exhibit.

There are many ways to stop a dog from jumping. If you put him in a cage, he can't jump. But that does nothing to teach the dog about what you want him to do. It helps to understand what the dog is trying to accomplish. In this case, it is probably to investigate a new person or object. Ultimately, we want the dog to be able to follow our directions in regards to the behavior. This comes from understanding, communication, and setting expectations to avoid a constant battle of what the dog wants and what we want.

Curtis Day: When a dog is jumping on you, the main motivation is wanting attention. Everyone's first instinct seems to be putting their hands on the dog and pushing them off. However, even though that is negative attention, the dog still receives it as the attention he was seeking. Essentially, the undesired jumping behavior is being rewarded. The best way to handle jumping is by starting with a strong "sit" command. When you come in the door, you immediately tell the dog to "sit" and you reinforce that behavior with a reward. This starts to set the boundaries. My dogs are allowed to jump on me, however, they must be invited first. When I give the command "up", they jump up gently to greet me. It is important to establish when the behavior is allowed and when it is not allowed. For example, you do not want the dog jumping on you when you come in with your hands full of groceries. Creating boundaries and expectations is a great way to handle jumping effectively.

Tom Longenecker: The easiest way to stop a dog from jumping is to rely on a solid foundation of obedience. For example, if your dog has a great "sit" command, that will be your number one tool for eliminating the jumping. If the dog is obediently holding that sit, he cannot be jumping on people in public or on guests in your home. This will also help with some of those social graces such as greeting people politely and not becoming too exuberant or overexcited. Relying on a skill that your dog has already mastered is a great way to eliminate undesired behaviors such as jumping.

Audra Mather: The first step in eliminating jumping behavior is limiting the options your dog has. The most simple and best training tool to help you is a leash. If your dog is on a leash, you can maintain control and not allow him to run and jump. Limiting his options will save you a lot of time and energy right off the bat. In addition, we want to make sure jumping behavior is never rewarded. You can also have other people get on board with this. For example, ask others to not pet your dog right away if he jumps on them. If the dog continues to see a pattern of not getting the attention he wants when he jumps, the behavior will decrease dramatically.

HP Parvizian: Oftentimes, our first response to a behavior such as jumping is going to be "No!", "Off!", or "Leave it!" Unfortunately, none of these commands are effective because the dog is just going to find other options. If he was jumping in front of you, he may change it up and jump behind you, to the side of you, or on a friend. We need to teach the dog what we would like him to do instead and give a very specific command such as "sit". "Sit" is one of the most powerful commands because by using it, we are telling the dog exactly what to do. Instead of pushing the dog off or ignoring him when he jumps, we give the dog a behavior to replace the jumping with. Never lose focus of what you WANT your dog to do when you are trying to tell him what you DON'T want him to do.

Lisa York: When dealing with a puppy that is jumping, make sure you are not rewarding them for the behavior. In the beginning, you are starting to learn your puppies' body language and when you see that he is going to jump, make an effort to keep him on the ground. As a dog gets older, dealing with jumping behavior is slightly different. Though we still do not want to reward undesired behavior, we also want to teach the dog how to manage his energy. By making sure that our energy level is kept low when we meet our dog, we can start to manage the jumping behavior. The best thing that happens to your dog all day is probably when you walk in the door. So we certainly understand his desire to jump and get excited. Creating leadership with your dog will also help alleviate the jumping. As the dog begins to recognize you as the leader of the family, you will find that the jumping will naturally decrease. Though jumping may sound like a very simple thing, there is a 15 prong approach to dealing with it at a holistic level. It isn't just about correcting and making the dog feel bad. It is about developing expectations about what is acceptable and what is not.

If you would like more information or to find a
"Sit Means Sit" near you, please visit
www.sitmeanssit.com

How Do I Get My Dog to Stop Pulling On the Leash?

Neil Cohen: The first step is to ask ourselves "What is the dog trying to accomplish?" In this case, it would be to investigate surroundings or get away from something. Much like operating a car, the dog needs to understand how the gas pedal operates. If he wants to move forward, there are steps that need to be taken. Dragging the person on the other end of the leash down the block is the undesired behavior. To achieve the desired behavior of walking side by side, we have to remember to not reinforce the negative. By moving forward every time the dog pulls, we are rewarding the behavior. If we stop doing this, the dog no longer finds enjoyment in it and the behavior will dissipate. Think of it like a brick wall. No matter how hard you push it with your forehead, it isn't going to move. You aren't going through it. You can sit there and bang your head against the wall, or you could find another way to conquer the wall. Maybe you could climb it, go around it, etc. You could explore new tools to accomplish the desired outcome. By being that wall and not moving when the dog pulls, we allow ourselves and our dog to find other acceptable options of moving forward together. Then we can reinforce these new desired behaviors and inevitably, see them more often.

Curtis Day: Simply stated, a brand new puppy or even an older dog that has never been exposed to a leash has to learn the expectations. A dog's natural instinct with a harness is to pull against that tension. It is our job to teach them about leash pressure and leash boundaries in order to have a dog that can successfully walk by our side.

Tom Longenecker: This is probably one of the most common questions that I hear. Again, making sure we have a solid foundation of obedience is key. Whether you are picking up a dog at eight weeks old or rescuing an older shelter dog, it is important to teach a really great "come" command. As long as this command is taught and reinforced properly, your dog should always be able to walk nicely next to you on a loose leash.

Audra Mather: The key here is not to reinforce the behavior. If the dog pulls, you do not move forward with the dog. There are many tools available that claim to help with leash pulling such as training harnesses, collars, etc. You really don't need any of that. Essentially, all you need to do is reward your dog for staying with you. Teach him that he will get to move forward only when he is by your side. Make it fun when he is with you. It is all about teaching boundaries and setting expectations for your dog.

HP Parvizian: Leash pulling is one of the most common concerns that we see. Walking your dog should be an enjoyable, relaxing activity that you both look forward to. But if your dog is constantly pulling on the leash, it becomes frustrating to the point where you don't want to do it anymore. Pulling on the leash is a habit that has been created and one of the biggest challenges is that our natural reaction is to pull back on that leash. This is called opposition reflex. The harder we pull back on the leash, the harder the dog will drive forward. This ultimately makes the problem worse. Some people unknowingly try to solve the issue by moving to a harness. A harness actually makes it more comfortable for the dog to pull and is obviously counterintuitive when it comes to stopping the pulling behavior.

The number one thing we can do is teach attention to our dog, by having him understand that the command "come" means to keep his head aligned with our body and move with attention and focus on us. We teach our clients to think about the walk in terms of individual steps. For each step you take, your dog should be taking another step to follow you. If you take one step and your dog takes off, stop right there and bring the dog back over to you. By reprogramming the walk into a system of steps, we are training the dog to have attention and stay next to us. It breaks the cycle of the dog pulling on the leash and you pulling back, creating a behavior that everyone has just come to regretfully accept.

Lisa York: Though we may not realize it, we are always rewarding our dog for pulling on the leash by moving forward. They are learning by cause and effect (if I pull, you move). We have to be conscious of the message we are sending to the dog by following them to each place they pull. The dog enjoys this because it is a natural opposition reflex.

The first thing you can do is use a flat collar instead of a harness. The harness actually creates the desire to pull. Each time the dog pulls, you should stop walking. The dog will turn around and certainly look at you as though you are crazy. If you are consistent, the dog will begin to understand that each time he pulls, you stop. You then can start to get erratic with your movements. Make left turns, right turns, go backwards. The dog will become so consumed with following your movements that he will forget about pulling and take his place behind you, following YOUR movements. Obviously, once you have this mastered, you can start taking walks with your dog like a normal person again.

If you would like more information or to find a "Sit Means Sit" near you, please visit www.sitmeanssit.com

How Do I Get My Dog to Stop Barking at Other Dogs and People?

Neil Cohen: Understanding what the dog is trying to accomplish goes a long way. Dogs do not have the language to tell us what they want. Barking is a very basic communication system. We can't put a translator on barks to decipher "Hey, there is a cat in the yard.", "Hey, I would like some food now." or "Hey, watch out!" It takes a deeper understanding of what the dog is trying to accomplish through barking. At the basic level, you could make the argument that 15,000 years ago we brought dogs into our families because they served a practical purpose...an alert system. If you go to sleep and the dog hears a predator outside, he is going to bark. If you take a dog hunting and he sees prey, he is going to bark. We have reinforced and bred this behavior for years. So as opposed to stopping it, we want to reinforce useful barking and get the dog to understand the difference between nuisance barking and purposeful barking. If we see the dog bark twice purposefully, instead of manically nonstop, it is important to reward that behavior.

Part of the problem is we have reinforcement systems around us all the time that encourage barking. For example, the mailman shows up at 10:00 am everyday to drop off the mail. The dog starts barking because he is protecting his house and thinks of the mailman as an intruder. The dog barks and barks and barks.....and the mailman LEAVES. We know he is leaving to simply move on to the next house, but the dog believes he is leaving because the barking drove him away. Thus, the undesired behavior is reinforced. We want to change the way our dog handles these situations. The best way to do that is to change the way we respond to the behavior. And always remember that understanding the "why" helps to come up with the "how".

Curtis Day: Dogs bark for a variety of reasons. Maybe they just want your attention. Perhaps they are trying to warn of danger. Maybe they want to play with another dog, or on the contrary, are barking at a cat because they do not like it and are attempting to frighten it away. In any case, the first thing we teach is how to get the dog's attention on the owner. A great command that I like to teach in this situation is "go". When the dog is barking, we can command "go", which means "go do something else." Commands force the dogs attention back to the owner and away from the undesired behavior or situation.

Tom Longenecker: There are many different reasons why a dog will bark. Pay attention to your dog's body language while they are barking to help determine the cause. Are they excited to go greet someone? Are they feeling defensive or uncomfortable? Did they get startled by something? The very best thing you can do is make sure your dog is well socialized. Expose them often to other people and animals. This will create a dog that is well-balanced and well-versed around different people and different places. It gives you the opportunity to show your dog how you expect them to react in a variety of situations and environments.

Audra Mather: For this type of situation, I recommend an "interrupt the behavior" approach. Again, the leash will be a great tool for this. If your dog is standing on the back of the couch barking at someone, all you have to do is grab the leash. Nothing to see here. Nothing to bark at. Immediately get your dog involved in something else to remove the focus from barking.

HP Parvizian: Barking is an interesting and fun problem to deal with. We see people come up with all different ways of trying to combat barking on their own. One of these ways is by using bark collars. The problem with these collars is that they do not tell the dog what behavior you want...only what you don't want. Bark collars create three different scenarios, with two of the three being useless when it comes to solving the problem. The ideal scenario is that the dog barks, receives the uncomfortable stimulation, and stops barking. This rarely ever happens. The second scenario is the dog barks, receives the stimulation, and has no idea what to do. He typically will move to one spot after another barking, trying to figure out which spot is the "right" one in which he won't receive the uncomfortable feeling. Thirdly, the dog barks and receives the stimulation. It startles him so much that he barks again. And again. And again. Now the dog is terrified AND still barking.

I say it often...communication and attention are the number one things we need when dealing with most undesirable behaviors. The more we yell at our dogs when they bark, the more they will continue to bark. It is like adding fuel to a fire. It is important to understand why dogs bark in the first place. Some dogs bark due to being reactive. This simply means they are trying to get another dog to go away. Some dogs bark because they are genuinely excited to see another dog. Dogs become vocal to show excitement. And again, the more energy we put into trying to stop that, the more excited they will get. Another common reason for barking is called "zone defense".

I also refer to this as the "postman bark". The postman arrives, the dog barks at him through the window and the postman goes away.. The dog thinks "I showed him." And so it continues day in and day out.

When the dog is inside his home, there is a barrier (such as a door or window), separating him from the postman and other dogs. When we go out for a walk, the problem exacerbates because the dog thinks "Here's my chance with no barriers to bark at these other people and dogs." I always tell my clients that "we will never fix a problem by ignoring it or rewarding it." For example, many people will try to walk their dog at odd hours of the night when no other dogs will be around. This is ignoring the issue. In addition, if we are constantly calling our dog back to us and giving him a treat to try to distract from barking, we are rewarding the behavior.

Instead, let's give the dog a job that we want him to do. My favorite behavior to teach in this situation is "Come". This tells the dog that whatever he is doing, he needs to stop and bring his head within petting distance of me. I am forcing his energy to redirect from the other dog to me. After he comes, I like to follow through with the "sit' command. This further requires his attention and focus.

Lisa York: The more we can train our dogs to focus on us, the better. The idea behind good training is that we want our dogs to be focused on us and what we have to offer instead of on the world around them. If your dog is barking, you should use your preferred "cease and desist" command and offer them something else to focus on.

The concept of "socialization" is very misleading. People think that this means their dog should love everyone, greet and jump up on everyone, and play with every other dog they come across. In fact, you want almost the exact opposite.

Ideally, your dog should treat every person and every other dog like a boring chair. They should be by your side until you give them the command and release them to go greet the new person or dog.

The baseline is getting your dog to focus on you, instead of thinking about what is in front of them causing them to bark. The more you can do that, the less the dog will bark because it will find more pleasure and satisfaction in what you have to offer.

If you would like more information or to find a "Sit Means Sit" near you, please visit
www.sitmeanssit.com

How Do I Potty Train
My New Puppy?

Neil Cohen: Now we are going to talk about the other side of reinforcement. In many of the previous examples, reinforcement is working against us and we have to be conscious of things like the dog pulling on the leash. We move forward and naturally reinforce this unwanted behavior. When it comes to potty training, dogs are getting reinforcement every time they eliminate. Not necessarily from you, but from the relief they feel when it happens. So when the puppy goes in the house, they are still getting that sense of relief. If we can use schedules, understand the physiology of when the dog has to go to the bathroom and get him to the place we want him to go, he can begin to pair the two.

In neurology, they say neurons that fire together, wire together. Going back to Pavlov, if every time the bell rings a dog gets food, the dog will start salivating when he hears a bell ring. So if every time he is taken to a certain spot and can eliminate and get satisfaction out of it, he is going to be more likely to want to go to that spot in the future. Using a schedule when puppies are young helps them to be successful. They need a schedule based on their age, bladder size, and when they last ate. We can use this to give them what they want, which is the opportunity to relieve themselves in the desired area and reward this behavior.

After this, we can teach them how to tell us more effectively when they have to go outside. Dogs are really great at communicating. For example, they will drop a toy on our lap when they want to play. They will grab the leash with their mouth when they want to go for a walk. As the potty schedule progresses, the dog will become better and better at indicating on his own when he understands the concept.

One of the biggest problems that I see when people are potty training their dogs is not following a schedule. So accidents happen and they're really not accidents. They're "on purposes". The puppy is not intentionally trying to soil your home. It is simply "I need to go to the bathroom, it feels good once I do, so I am going to do that again." With our busy schedules, sometimes we miss the signs or aren't as consistent as we would like to be. The better you are at sticking to a potty schedule, the more you can reinforce the desired behavior. Consistency becomes habit.

Curtis Day: The two key elements to potty training are maintaining a strict schedule and crate training. Limit the crate to the size of your dog at first and upgrade to a larger one as the dog grows. Make sure to give the dog food and water in the crate so the dog starts to associate it with being a positive place. Then set a consistent schedule as to when you will take your dog out for potty breaks so you can reward them for going outside. It is important to remember that we do not punish bad behavior. Dogs are not able to distinguish between negative and positive attention. We could be unintentionally rewarding bad behavior by attention through punishment. For this reason, ONLY reward the behavior you want to see. In most cases, potty training is failed by the people. They often miss cues or are not consistent with keeping a schedule. Pay attention to your dog and get to know his cues so you can both be successful.

Tom Longenecker: Potty training is a big concern for obvious reasons. Nobody likes the idea of accidents in the house. However, remember to have realistic expectations when dealing with a puppy. You are guaranteed at least a couple accidents in the potty training phase. The best way to go about potty training is to make sure that you are utilizing a management system such as a crate, kennel, or even a small pen. This restricts the dog from sneaking off to a corner of the house if you aren't able to give your full attention to them. A good schedule is another key element to potty training. Just like children, dogs thrive on structure. Creating a schedule of feeding times, potty times, and even times that you offer water can really help a dog who might be struggling with potty training. After all, if we control what is going in, we can help control what is going out.

Audra Mather: I am a big fan of crate training a puppy. Any time your puppy is not in the crate, I recommend keeping him on a leash. I refer to this as "tethering". Literally attach the leash to your belt. Everywhere you go, the puppy goes with you. This way, he can't sneak off and have an accident when your eyes aren't on him. With housebreaking comes a little bit of safety training as well. Tethering will also prevent the puppy from getting into something that could injure him.

In addition to the crate and tethering, a schedule is an absolute must. It is very important to stick to this schedule. If it helps, set little alarms or a kitchen timer to be reminded to take the puppy out. Take him to the same place in the yard and choose the best treats to bring with you for positive reinforcement. It should be a unique treat...something with high value that the dog does not receive everyday. You can use chicken, turkey, or my personal favorite...string cheese. String cheese is great because it is easy to grab on your way out the door.

Make sure you stand in the exact same place each time you take the puppy out. Only give him the radius of the leash. When the puppy goes, say "Good puppy, go potty" and reward him with that high value treat. Don't allow there to be any lag between the puppy going potty and receiving the treat. We really need to be consistent in order for potty training to start off on the right foot.

What if the puppy does not go? You have been standing around for five minutes and the puppy does not go potty. Take him back inside and put him in the crate for fifteen minutes. Set a timer if you need to. After the time is up, bring the puppy back outside to that same spot. Don't forget your treats! Times that puppy should be taken outside are after naps, after he has been running around playing for awhile, and 10-15 minutes after eating or drinking. Providing food and water on a schedule will also help you and your puppy be successful.

If you ever start to have potty issues with an older dog, it is necessary to start all over from the beginning. Pretend you have a new puppy again. An experienced trainer can help you with this process and provide you with tips, tools, and encouragement.

HP Parvizian: We receive many calls about potty training and marking. Many people will say "My dog is housebroken, but he is still marking." We treat this exactly the same as a dog who needs to be potty trained starting back at square one. I have a little joke that I tell my clients when it comes to potty training. My secret for success and the FASTEST way to potty train your dog starts with rolling up newspapers or magazines really tight, duct taping them together and placing these rolls all over your house. The tighter and stronger, the better. Anytime you find a spot in the house where your dog peed or pooped without you knowing, pick up the roll and hit yourself in the head as hard as you can and say "I should have been watching my dog." Because when a dog has an accident without us knowing, it is OUR fault, not theirs. I compare it to giving a two or three year old child a marker and paper and walking out of the room. I will probably come back to a marker mural all over my wall, which would be my fault for not watching the child. It is my job to teach that child or puppy the expectations of the household.

Housebreaking a puppy is laborious. I always recommend to start out with crating and having your puppy on a leash anytime they are not in the crate. Crating a dog is very important when it comes to teaching him how to hold it indoors. As an added bonus, crating protects the puppy and prevents him from destroying your house. Any time your dog is not in the crate, I recommend that he is on a leash attached to you. Life is a lot less stressful when you are not wondering where your puppy is and what he is getting into every second of the day. On a 15 foot leash, you can keep a close eye on your dog while you go about your daily routine. Maybe you will notice him circling, sniffing, or squating and can take him out to the appropriate place in the yard. The puppy won't be able to make a mistake that you haven't seen and you will always have the opportunity to teach.

With a very young puppy, be sure to take him outside every hour to the same spot on a leash. He should not have freedom to run around and chase squirrels. We want to teach him to "potty" on command, just like "come" or "sit". And as soon as the potty happens, the celebrating begins with praise and rewards. Now the dog can have some freedom to run around for a bit. He can also enjoy some freedom inside the house on the leash. If the puppy did not go, bring him back to the crate and try again five or ten minutes later.

Clients often ask about the best way to start expanding the dog's area within the home. I don't immediately move the puppy from the crate to full access of the home. I simply expand the area around the crate by building a larger enclosure. I make the puppy earn the freedom by getting better and better at going outside. If the puppy makes a mistake or has an accident, I don't immediately take them back to the crate. I just move back to the last enclosure size that was successful.

Offering food and water on a schedule is another tactic that will make the potty training process go more smoothly. Don't ever "free feed" your puppy. A young puppy should ideally be fed three times a day and taken outside ten minutes after eating. Similarly, offer water every hour and take the puppy out a few minutes after drinking. Creating this type of schedule makes it easier to predict when your puppy will need to go and will minimize accidents.

A common concern about potty training comes from my clients who are at work all day long. There are two possible solutions here. First of all, you can install a dog door that leads to a safe, enclosed area outside where you would like the dog to go potty. Then back your crate up to the inside area of the dog door. This allows the dog to leave his crate to use the bathroom and come back inside to relax as he wishes. A second option would be to create a kenneled area around your crate inside the home. Put down a couple puppy pads so the dog can leave his crate to go potty. The whole process may take a bit longer, but I would rather have it done the right way and not have the owner be stressed about having to go to work.

Remember that every dog owner has a unique lifestyle. Our goal is to teach the owner what they can do differently to get the desired behavior from the dog. Especially when it comes to potty training, it is important to have patience just as we do with our human children.

Lisa York: We get people that want us to potty train their dogs all the time. Here is a key point to remember: A dog can be perfectly well behaved in one environment and do something silly somewhere else because he simply does not understand the concept. In the very beginning stages of potty training, there are two things you need to focus on: management and confinement. Many people will believe that potty training is going very fast and that their dog is potty trained way before it actually is since the dog has not made a mistake. The real reason ends up being that the owner has been so on top of it, the dog has not been given the opportunity to make a mistake.

The first step in potty training is teaching your dog to be crated. We have many techniques to create a very positive experience and make the crate a place that your dog actually enjoys. I breed German Shepherds and typically have all of my puppies housebroken by the age of 10 weeks. When outside of the crate, I keep my puppies on a leash which is attached to me at all times. There is no correction in the process of potty training a puppy, only redirection. When the puppy is next to you, it allows you to pay attention and always have the opportunity to remind him where you want him to go, as opposed to him sneaking off and going behind a chair. You begin to learn the potty patterns of your puppy and how often he should be given opportunities after eating or drinking.

As a general rule, if the puppy is not with you, he should be in the crate. This is for safety and potty training purposes. A puppy can generally be expected to hold their bladder or bowels an hour for each month of life until they are about eight months old. We don't ever recommend leaving your dog for more than eight hours.

If you would like more information or to find a "Sit Means Sit" near you, please visit www.sitmeanssit.com

How Can I Get My Dog to Stop Chewing On Things?

Neil Cohen: We always start with the end in mind. Why is my dog chewing? Does it feel good? Does it taste good? Does it get your attention? It really all depends on what your dog is getting out of it. For example, your dog grabs a sock. Let's assume for a moment the dog does not like the taste or smell of the sock. But every time he picks up a sock, you chase him around to get the sock back. He discovers that no matter how busy you are, he can immediately receive your attention by confiscating the sock. Inadvertently, you are rewarding the behavior with your reaction.

We also must remember that this behavior does not warrant a punishment. Unless there is a danger, we are not trying to make a connection. So it is best not to punish, but also not to reward either. Redirecting the dog's focus to something else or practicing some obedience training is a great distraction. You can also make minor changes to create a desired outcome. For example, the dog is constantly chewing on the woodwork. A simple solution would be a spritz of bitter apple spray, making the taste unappealing to the dog. Perhaps it is that your dog really just wants attention. Engage him in a game of chase or fetch to alleviate his desire to get attention (even if it is negative attention) from chewing on household items. It is all about teaching your dog a different way to get what he wants.

Curtis Day: Chewing behavior can be a sign of a couple different things. First of all, if it is a young puppy, they could simply be teething. Just like babies, puppy's find relief for sore gums through chewing. In the case of an older dog, it is typically boredom. In either situation, make sure to offer your dog plenty of acceptable items to chew on such as toys and chew sticks. Also keep in mind that obedience training is great because it allows dogs to use that mental energy toward something productive.

Tom Longenecker: Many times destructive behaviors such as chewing can be due to lack of mental stimulation. Your dog is bored and looking for things to do, so stealing socks sounds fun. Dogs will make their own fun if you aren't providing it for them. Most of the time, we won't find their idea of fun and games very appealing. It is important to provide opportunities that mentally challenge your dog. Working with a trainer on obedience, offering fun new games, or teaching new skills are a great way for dogs to burn off some of that mental energy. When in doubt, you can always use a management system such as a crate, kennel, or pen. This ensures the safety of your dog while you are away and protects your cords and furniture from damage.

Audra Mather: Keep in mind that dogs are naturally drawn to chew on items that smell like us. Dogs often go after remotes because we had food on our hands and then touched the remote. They steal socks and underwear because they find comfort in the smell of their human companions. Very simply, make sure to pick up your stuff and put it away. Ideally, we do not want dogs chewing on our belongings so don't tempt them with clutter all over the floor. In addition, provide your dog with many appropriate things to chew on such as bones, toys, etc.

If you are having a big problem with chewing, an experienced dog trainer can help you. I often go into homes and help families who are having significant issues with chewing or other undesirable behaviors. It's all about helping to manage the chaos and stress of running a household by making sure we are doing things to set the dog up for success. If there are small children, this provides a great opportunity to teach them about putting away their toys. After the first teddy bear gets chewed up by the dog, the children will certainly want to take responsibility for their things. Tethering your dog to you and limiting areas he has access to by closing doors can also help significantly with the temptation to chew.

HP Parvizian: At the end of the day, chewing is a way for a dog to release extra energy they have in their mind and body. In the case of a young puppy, teething causes him to search for a way to alleviate that pain. The number one solution to chewing, even if your dog is housebroken, is to kennel him. Create a space where the dog cannot cause any damage to furniture, tables, and cords. If you think about it, we do the same thing with small children. We put up baby gates to give them a safe place to play. The safety of your puppy should always be the main concern.

Once again, when it comes to chewing, we need to focus on giving the dog something else to do instead. For example, let's look at a dog who is constantly sticking his head in the trash. Our initial reaction would be to start yelling and screaming for the dog to get away from the trash can. But ultimately, we do not want our dog to be afraid of the trash can. We want our dog to be confident in any situation and any area of his home.

This is where teaching behavior comes into play. When the dog goes for the trash again, call him over to you and make him "sit" in an area by himself. Upon release, he runs back to the trash. Call him over again. Make him "sit." Repeat the process until the dog no longer makes a beeline for the garbage. He will begin to make the connection that if he sticks his head in the trash, he loses his freedom to move around the house and has to sit. Simultaneously, he will make the connection that sitting, laying, or walking by the trash is fine and will not develop an irrational fear.

Going back to chewing and the need for expelling energy, I have an interesting fact to share. Another reason the "sit" command is so valuable is because it requires more energy to hold a 30 minute sit than to complete a 6 mile run. Every muscle is engaged and tense, the dog has to hold his head high, and maintain posture. He is also forced to use the mental energy to remember to sit...not run around, not jump on the couch, not bark at the window. The benefits of teaching commands are twofold. By using up this physical and mental energy, we are eliminating the need to chew. Secondly, we are developing that focus and attention perfecting commands that can be used in a variety of situations.

Lisa York: If you have a dog that is past the teething stage and they are no longer soothing their gums or helping erupt a tooth, chewing behavior is a direct result of boredom. Oftentimes, the solution is as simple as giving them something to be entertained by or a way to expend their energy. This can be achieved through toys and walks. Typically, as dogs age, chewing is a sign of growth. Essentially, a dog is providing acupuncture for his mind and energy through chewing. Taking him for a walk, run, or playing ball will release this energy and the chewing behavior will dissipate.

Most importantly, we cannot forget to teach the dog right from wrong. People often remember to scold and remove the undesired item from the dog, but forget to provide him with something acceptable to chew on. For example, if your dog is chewing on an electrical cord, remove the cord, say "No", and give him a bone or a Kong toy instead. In this way, the dog is learning what items are allowed to be chewed on.

If you would like more information or to find a
"Sit Means Sit" near you, please visit
www.sitmeanssit.com

How Can I Get My Dog to Like Other Dogs, Animals and People?

Neil Cohen: First of all, what and who the dog decides to like is completely up to them. Let's look at an example. Let's assume you hate roller coasters. I love them. We both sit in the front row of the roller coaster and we go up and down and left and right a hundred miles an hour. The experience is exactly the same physically, but mentally we are going to have very different perspectives. I can give you a million dollars to go on the roller coaster time after time and if there is value to you, you will probably do it. But that doesn't mean you are going to like it. And again, that would be up to you.

So we want to focus more on what the response of the dog is to people or things that he doesn't like. If your dog becomes aggressive and tries to attack another dog, we are going to teach him how to respond differently. We certainly can't expect a dog to change how he feels about a certain situation. But if we go back to that roller coaster example, and I am still paying you a million a week to go on it, you might decide that you haven't died yet and you could actually be enjoying it. So we start to pair these two elements. You may ride one willingly tomorrow for free because you have changed the perception in your mind. But I had to bring you to that place in a safe, connected way. The same goes for attempting to change the way your dog feels about certain people or things.

Curtis Day: I always recommend early socialization. As soon as possible, get your dog around other dogs and people. Schedule some puppy playdates. Let your dog experience doggy daycare. It can be very beneficial to find an experienced trainer that offers these types of social settings so that they can observe your dog. People can often mistake playing for aggression. Along with socialization, start to work on polite interaction early. For example, if you are walking your dog through Home Depot, certainly allow people to come up and pet your dog. But make your dog "sit" before he receives the attention. Do not allow him to jump. Setting those expectations early is key.

Tom Longenecker: It is a common misconception that our dogs need to be best friends with everyone and everything. Just like with people, that doesn't have to be the case. Some dogs are going to be social butterflies, while others are going to be a little more introverted and that's completely okay. The most important thing is that our dogs are taught to tolerate other people and animals with politeness. When it comes to socialization, we just need to make sure that our dog feels confident in an environment with other dogs. Ultimately, we want other people or animals in any situation to be able to have a safe, healthy interaction with our dog.

Audra Mather: It all starts with proper socialization from early on. When you have a puppy, you want to expose your puppy to all sorts of people and things. We want the puppy to see people on crutches, on scooters, on bikes, in wheelchairs and pushing strollers. Bring the puppy around all different types of people including men with beards, small children, and little old ladies. The more exposure the puppy gets to all of these things when he is young, the less likely he will be to develop fears later. Just like children, dogs go through developmental stages including various levels of fear, so it is important to begin exposure young.

In the case of a dog who is fearful of other dogs and is growling, barking, or lashing out on the leash, I always recommend getting professional help from a trainer. This is called leash reactivity and is a very common issue. In most cases, aggression stems from fear. A trainer can help you and your dog work through this in a safe, effective manner. If a dog has had a fearful or negative experience with other dogs in the past, we can absolutely help rehab that dog.

You can stop this fear from occuring by being selective about your dog's playmates from the very beginning. Provide positive interactions and look for signs of being bullied or terrified by another dog. Places like dog parks do not always provide positive interactions. Many people use dog parks for the wrong reasons. They have dogs that are wild and out of control, and turn them loose on the park to run off some of that energy. Just like humans, not every dog is going to get along. It is very difficult to gauge interactions when a pack of dogs is running high speed through a dog park in the opposite direction from you. By keeping our dogs at a close distance with other non-aggressive playmates early on, we can set them up for confident encounters with dogs in the future.

HP Parvizian: We need to look at dogs the same way we look at people. There are all different personality types...timid, fearful, aggressive, unsure, excited, confident. A dog's personality will determine how he reacts around people and other dogs. Just like humans, we cannot expect a dog to be a huge fan of everyone and everything in his life. But a dog has to learn to TOLERATE everyone. We all have people that we must learn to tolerate, whether it be coworkers, family members, or friends of our significant others. The focus should never be to get our dogs to love everyone. For a dog who is timid and afraid, I want that dog to hold a nice sit near the other person or dog and tolerate being there. Eventually, the dog will become more comfortable in this situation.

The same goes for a dog with reactivity and aggression. You want him to give up that desire to "fight or flight" and focus attention on you with a command. Think of it like two siblings who are fighting. The more you try to force them to be friends, the more they will battle. Have them sit near each other and tolerate each other. Let them know that the behavior expected from them is to be cordial, well-mannered children. Eventually they will let their guards down, as will an aggressive dog.

All of this will help in creating a more relaxed dog. It takes much of the weight off of the dog's shoulders when it comes to deciding how he should handle a particular situation. The dog can now turn his attention to the owner and be guided on decisions and the creation of new behaviors. Owners feel more confident about entering social situations with their dog. They now have the power to rely on behaviors and commands in order to diffuse any potentially negative situations. Many of my clients who previously could never be around other people or dogs are now happily enjoying time at the dog park with confident, well-adjusted animals.

Lisa York: Dogs are just like people in that they have their own personalities and their own preferences. If you have a dog that doesn't particularly love to be around people or other dogs, I always advise to be an advocate for your dog. Don't put your dog in a situation that would make him uncomfortable. If I had a dog that didn't get enjoyment from being around other dogs, I would avoid places like the dog park.

Regardless, the expectation still remains that our dogs must be polite. We should be teaching them not to bark and growl at other dogs and people, while also respecting the fact that they may not want to be pet by a stranger and creating those boundaries. Again, be an advocate for your dog.

Barking at other dogs and humans often stems from fear. We can help our dogs with this by putting them in situations that build confidence, where the owner "has their back." For example, if your dog doesn't like to interact with other dogs, still take him to the dog park. But hang out just outside of the park and play ball with your dog or take him for a walk. Your dog is still being flooded with the experience of being around other dogs, but also being encouraged knowing that he is going to have fun with you and doesn't have to worry about the other dogs in his face.

If you would like more information or to find a "Sit Means Sit" near you, please visit www.sitmeanssit.com

Should I Allow My Dog On the Furniture?

Neil Cohen: I always say this is a personal choice until it is a problem. What do I mean by that? First of all, there's nothing wrong with dogs being on the furniture unless you don't want dogs on your furniture. Some people are more than happy to have their dogs on their couch or in their bed and even prefer it that way. I joke all the time that dog hairs are my favorite accessories.

The only time this becomes a problem is when you don't want it to happen and it still happens. If your dog is battling you for ownership of the couch, the problem isn't the couch. The problem is your relationship. It all boils down to leadership. Displaying leadership allows the dog to understand where he can and cannot be.

Let's put it in the context of children. If your daughter walks into the kitchen, opens the cabinet, takes a whole bunch of Oreos and starts shoving them in her mouth 15 minutes before dinner, she obviously doesn't understand good eating habits or what the rules of the house are. In order to have our children be capable of making good decisions, we have to make decisions for them in the very beginning. Then we give them the leeway and reserve the right to overrule those decisions. Ultimately, they start to make those decisions on their own more and more consistently.

For example, now your daughter pulls out the Oreos and you turn around and say "Honey, we are going to have dinner in

15 minutes. Please put those away. Those are for dessert." She says "Ok, mom. I didn't know we were having dinner now. Let me help you set the table." You were able to overrule the decision with no conflict and you both move forward together with an understanding of "when" and "how".

This brings us back to the dog and the couch. We want the dog to understand if he is welcome on the couch and when he is welcome on the couch. Some owners require their dogs to wait for an invitation such as "Ok, you can come up on the couch now." Otherwise, the dog is not permitted up. Does your dog understand the rules? Is he willing to follow them? Or does he turn around and eat all the Oreos in the cabinet? You know you have good leadership if your dog accepts the rules of the household. Leadership is not establishing force or fear. It is letting your dog know that you have his best interests at heart.

Curtis Day: Allowing your dog on the furniture is a personal preference. It is entirely up to you and what you are comfortable with. In my home, the dogs are allowed on the furniture ONLY when I invite them up. If I am sitting on the couch watching TV, they will sit at my feet and look up at me, asking for permission. This is a direct result of setting those early boundaries and expectations.

Tom Longenecker: Very simply, it's your dog. It's your house. It's your furniture. If you just got a brand new expensive leather sofa, you may not want your dog clawing it up or getting mud and hair all over it. If you are a dog person like myself, you may not have any issue with it at all. The most important thing is that you are remaining consistent with expectations and that your dog clearly understands the rules of the house. Some people choose to allow their dog on only one item of furniture...a special place where they can hang out with their dog and the dog understands this is "their spot." Whatever you decide, just make sure your dog has a place where they can comfortably relax and you feel comfortable and confident knowing your dog understands and respects the rules you have created.

Audra Mather: Most dog owners enjoy snuggling their dog on the couch or in bed, myself included. I believe in taking a "permissive" approach, meaning my dogs can come up next to me only when invited. They won't go running into Grandma's house and leaping onto her furniture, because they know it would never fly with me. Personally, I love all my dogs in the bed at once. But only when I ask them, otherwise I would never get any sleep!

HP Parvizian: I have one simple rule when it comes to furniture. My dogs are allowed on every piece of furniture in my home...bed, sofa, dining room table, kitchen counter. But first, they must be invited. Similarly, I am allowed to be at every house in the world if I am invited. Obviously, I would never invite my dogs on the dining room table and therefore, they will never do it. This is a direct result of the training and expectations that I have set since the very beginning. If I am sitting on the sofa, my dogs will look at me, almost asking for permission. If I invite them, they willingly jump up and hang out with dad. If I do not give them permission at that moment, they wander off or lay down on the floor at my feet.

This permissive behavior is great because it can also translate to other situations like moving through doorways and entering cars. My dogs wait for my command to enter and exit doors as well. They don't rush out an open front door unless they are invited to do so. The same goes with the car. I have two small children and I don't want my dogs jumping on top of them as soon as the car door opens. Once again, they must be invited to hop in the car. Creating these types of simple rules and expectations results in a stress free environment for humans and dogs alike.

Lisa York: Allowing your dog on the furniture is an individual choice. With that being said, the dog should have the understanding that he needs to be "invited" on the furniture. If you always allow your dog on the couch at his own free will, he will never understand why you kick him off the couch when company comes over. Personally, all of my dogs are allowed on the couch with permission. They have to look up at me and wait for me to say "Yes". If I say "No, go lay down.", they have learned to go to their bed or crate. You should always maintain control if you make the decision to let your dogs on the furniture.

Also keep in mind, your puppy is going to grow. If you bring home a 10-15 pound German Shepherd puppy and allow him on the couch, he will not understand why he suddenly is not allowed anymore at 85 pounds. Make sure you are consistent from the beginning and know whether or not you will want a large dog on your furniture so you don't have to take this privilege away from them in the future. Just like children, dogs do best when they understand the rules, routines, and order of the household.

If you would like more information or to find a "Sit Means Sit" near you, please visit www.sitmeanssit.com

How Do I Make the Time for Training?

Neil Cohen: Most people look at dog training as a herculean task. The typical person says to himself "I have two kids, each of them plays three sports, I have a house to take care of and a job. And now I have to find the time to train a dog?" The good news is, training really doesn't take much. Dogs learn best 10-15 minutes at a time. If we do that once or twice a day with consistency and set simple goals, training becomes much less daunting. You can incorporate training into almost anything you normally do with your dog. Even a game of fetch in the yard can turn into a training session, by having the dog work on sitting calmly in front of you, then releasing him, and then rewarding him. I always advocate for 10-15 minutes once or twice a day because it is achievable and will produce great results for you and your dog.

Curtis Day: Training isn't something you have to make time for. At Sit Means Sit, we encourage the "train as you live" approach. Anything that you do with your dog throughout the day is a training opportunity. Everything from feeding your dog, to taking them outside to go potty, to playing with them can be turned into a few minutes of training time. Don't look at training as a task. It is something that should happen naturally and frequently in your daily routine.

Tom Longenecker: When it comes to dog training, we are training in the moment. A big part of my job is teaching people how to train their dog in small aspects of everyday life. Our schedules are often hectic and don't allow large free chunks of time during the day. It is easy to incorporate training into the small windows of time we have available. For example, you can have your dog hold a sit while you are enjoying your morning cup of coffee. You can practice the "heel" command while your dog follows you around the house during chores. You can practice doorway boundaries while you are going in and out to let them use the bathroom, check the mail, or go for a walk. These are all excellent opportunities to do some training with your dog that continuously occur in your daily life.

Audra Mather: Finding the time is where we make it easy on people. By practicing a "train as you live" philosophy, you simply go about your day and incorporate training into the things you are already doing anyway. For example, if you are making dinner and you don't want your dog underfoot in the kitchen, you practice the command to have him wait outside the door. In a perfect world, everyone would have a solid extra hour each day to devote to their dog. If you can incorporate a couple of 15 minute blocks into your day, that is wonderful. Interacting and building a relationship with your dog inevitably leads to teachable moments.

HP Parvizian: Time is the one thing that makes everyone in this world equal. We all have 24 hours in a day. One thing I hear from my clients quite often is that they don't have the time for training. I am going to show you how to make time. I never want my clients to leave their life to train the dog. I want them to bring the dog INTO their life. Sit Means Sit focuses on a "train as you live" mentality. If I have laundry to do, I will have my dog hold a sit while I fold. If I have trash to take out, I will have the dog follow the "come" command with the distraction of smelly trash in my hand. To familiarize your dog with a new baby, call him to you during diaper changes. Have him hold a sit while you change the baby. Release him when it is time to throw the diaper away. Simple daily tasks like these offer excellent training opportunities and build structure within the household.

Dog training consists of three "Ds"...distance, duration, and distraction. Distance refers to things like how far a dog can walk and how far you can walk away from your dog. Duration is describing how long your dog can hold a sit or how long he can stay before being released. And then there is distraction. What else is going on in the world? We want our dogs to be able to hold attention even with distractions present. Mastering the three "Ds" can occur through practicing in those "train as you live" moments for just minutes a day.

Lisa York: Training is a lifelong process. You really should never stop. Let's compare it to going to the gym. If you want results, you don't go to the gym one time. You go consistently. The same goes for training your dog. Consistency is key. This is exactly why we like to use the phrase "train as you live". If you are having dinner, instruct your dog to go lay down on his bed. This is training. While you are spending time outside, throw a ball to your dog and have him bring it back. This is training. It doesn't have to be an extensive, planned out training session. It should happen organically as you go about your day to day routine. Whenever you are with your dog, you are sending messages about what they can and cannot do. They are looking at you, observing your body language, and following what you do. Essentially, you are training all day long without even realizing it.

If you would like more information or to find a
"Sit Means Sit" near you, please visit
www.sitmeanssit.com

What Is the Most Important Thing People Should Consider When Choosing a Dog Trainer?

Neil Cohen: Dog training is not transactional. It is not like going to the supermarket, grabbing a carton of milk, handing your card to the clerk and walking out. It takes a solid relationship and connection between you, your dog, and the trainer. Make sure the trainer really stands behind what they are doing. A good trainer will have a system and steps to get the job done and will help you keep it going for the life of your dog. Inevitably, over the years, things change. Your dog gets older, you may move into a new house, or have more children. We develop a strong foundation with you and your dog in the beginning and provide you with the tools to keep training throughout life's many stages. We like to think of our training as a "cradle to the grave" type of process. We begin by training the dog, overlapped by training the handler. Then we move into a program that provides controlled distraction so the dog can practice in a group setting. Ultimately, we want the owner to leave feeling that they have an easy, effective system to implement in their daily lives.

Curtis Day: The most important thing is to find a trainer with experience and credentials. For example, here in Wyoming, there are no regulations on dog trainers. Anyone could say they are a trainer without having any credentials whatsoever. Make sure you are dealing with someone who has an insured, legitimate business and a high level of experience.

Secondly, a dog trainer that has a facility is a huge plus and something that would stand out to me as a prospective client. In Wyoming, where we have snow three quarters of the year, it is not possible to do very many group classes outside. Our beautiful indoor facility allows us to offer training for the life of your dog, 365 days a year.

Tom Longenecker: The number one thing to look for is how well behaved the trainer's dog is. That will give you an excellent idea of what the trainer's final product will look like. After all, this is a dog that the trainer lives with 24/7. If their dog is not displaying behaviors that you would like to see in your dog, they might not be the best fit for you. In addition, dog training is very intimate and personal. You certainly want someone that you and your dog feel a strong connection with. There are many different personalities and styles when it comes to dog trainers. Take the time to find the right match for you. You want someone who will help you to replicate the strategies into your daily life. But you also want someone that you can have fun with and get results with.

Audra Mather: First of all, make sure the training style, personality, and skill set match what you are looking for. Meet the trainer in person and ask to see an example of a dog they have trained from start to finish. Watch videos and client testimonials. Take a tour of the facility so that you can assess things like cleanliness and observe other dogs in training.

Anybody can talk, but a good trainer needs to show you proven results.

HP Parvizian: There are a lot of great dog trainers out there. Every dog trainer you meet should be able to work your dog right there in front of you. I want my potential clients to see what kind of techniques I use and what I am able to accomplish with their dog in a few minutes. From a trainer standpoint, I like being able to gauge temperament, behavioral patterns, and learning ability in person to better meet the needs of the dog and owner. It is important that the owner is able to envision themselves following through with the type of training I offer. It doesn't matter how great the system is if the owner will be unable to replicate it at home.

When searching for a qualified professional, also be sure to observe the trainer's personal dogs off leash and around distractions. I compete my dogs nationally in many arenas including dock diving and between myself and my colleagues, our dogs have been in the top ranks of almost every sport out there. If we can't "walk the walk" with our own dogs, how are we going to help yours? Great trainers should have happy, confident dogs that are excellent at following commands off leash with distractions.

Lisa York: A trainer with good communication skills is very important. Not only is the professional training your dog, they are also helping YOU to train your dog. For this reason, effective communication with the human at the other end of the leash is just as important as communication with the dog. We want you to be able to take your dog home and achieve the same results.

Secondly, look for a trainer that views the dog as a whole. It is important to find someone who has a balanced approach to training and takes all behaviors into account, not just one. Choose someone who interacts with your dog well and uses a variety of techniques that are easy and enjoyable for you to learn and implement as well.

If you would like more information or to find a
"Sit Means Sit" near you, please visit
www.sitmeanssit.com

Meet the Experts

Neil Cohen

Master Trainer

Sit Means Sit

My Amazing Journey...from Frustrated Dog Owner to Master Trainer

Hi, my name is Neil Cohen. I have been a dog person my whole life. Even after being bit as a child, I never can remember a moment that I wasn't drawn to dogs.

When I was 5, we moved to the suburbs and adopted our first dog. I can remember everything about that day. We went to Bide-a-wee on Long Island and walked the aisles, looking at all the sad, mad, happy and downright crazy dogs. Everyone was barking and howling, except for one. We found this beautiful, calm border collie mix. She was black and white, and her tail never stopped wagging for a second. That was her, our dog. And we named her Fluffy (pretty original, right?)

Fluffy was a great dog. Aside from stealing socks and pulling off my brother's diaper, she was perfect. Times were different then; we just opened the door and she ran around the neighborhood. Somehow, she always came back when you called. Just like kids knew that the streetlights were a signal to head for home, she did her business and came home for dinner.

As we grew up, we got a few more dogs, but Fluffy was our constant companion. She never had any real training and, in our eyes, never needed any. We lost her after 17 wonderful years and will always have her in our hearts.

When I grew up and moved into my first suburban home, I felt it was time for our family to have a bigger dog. One I could hike with, one that would keep the bad guys away. And we adopted Cody. A strong, confident year and a half year-old boxer with virtually no training. He was a sweetheart but barely even housebroken. He was found wandering the streets in South Carolina and somehow wound up in a Cocker Spaniel rescue. Well, I figured "how hard could it be?" I mean, I had dogs my whole life...I could train this one. It was a disaster. Everyone that walked in was greeted with enthusiasm. So much enthusiasm that they were knocked down stairs, bumped into walls and covered with slobber. He chewed toys, chased chipmunks and walking him could have been an Olympic sport.

But I was committed to making this work. I watched videos and read books. He learned all kinds of tricks, but he still couldn't control his enthusiasm and we were frustrated to say the least.

Then, by chance, I happened upon some YouTube videos of Fred Hassen, the founder of Sit Means Sit. Fred had built a huge following posting a new dog training video every day. Sit Means Sit wasn't yet a franchise, but Fred was sharing his unique method of attention-based training with the world and showing trainers how to use his system. Now, I wasn't looking to be a dog trainer. I had a successful business that I enjoyed. Fortunately, Fred was the sharing type and I was able to learn enough to make positive changes in Cody's behavior. We were hiking off leash and people could visit us. All was grand.

Eventually, a Sit Means Sit franchise opened in Fairfield, CT by an amazing trainer named Allen Burnsworth. We quickly became friends and Allen took me under his wing. The plan was that I would train dogs on the weekend in Westchester, saving him the drive from Connecticut.

Like many things, plans don't always work out as you expect. Allen was given the opportunity to take over a Master Territory on the West Coast and wanted to sell his franchise. Of course, he told me this at 2:00 am on a Thursday. It took me all of 17 seconds to decide this was what I was meant to do. Four days later I flew to Las Vegas to begin my training with Fred. Intensive isn't the word for it. Our days were long, 10-12 hours of mostly hands-on instruction. We spent hours at the shelters, training dogs without names, helping to get them adopted. After a month of tutelage, I headed home to start my new career.

Five years later, training hundreds of dogs and transforming lives, I've never looked back. Dog training has given me almost everything I could have dreamed of. I met my wife, Jamie, through her dog Sarge. I was given the gift of time with my kids, Justin and Kayla. And I have an enormous pack. Three of my own: Pepper, Sarge, and Eddie, and all of my client's dogs, as I consider each one of them part of my family. Together with my dogs we have brought smiles to Veterans (through K9 Caring Angels Therapy Dogs), we entertained tens of thousands of fans as the Batdog for the New York Boulder's baseball team (Pepper is the first and only dog to Batdog in a professional All-Star game), and, most importantly, we have helped our clients to lead happier lives with their dogs.

All because I was a frustrated dog owner.

Tell us about your business and the types of people/dogs that you help.

Neil Cohen: Most often, I help people that remind me of myself when I first became a dog owner. These people are extremely frustrated, feeling they know how to get the training done but just can't get it done. Before I became a dog trainer, I adopted a dog that challenged me. I was certain I could succeed with him, but it was a constant struggle. He was knocking my children down, pulling people on the leash, and exhibiting several nuisance behaviors. They were not necessarily bad or aggressive behaviors, just behaviors that had to be fixed in order for us to enjoy being a family together. We see many people in the same boat. They have absolutely wonderful dogs, but they may be impossible to walk a mile with on a leash or are constantly jumping on people. Not terrible behaviors, but ones that decrease the pleasure of having a dog.

The other side of the coin is people that come to us with serious behavioral issues. These are the people who are afraid to leave their homes with their dog or are afraid of the dog harming their children or causing alarm to their neighbors. We see them at their wit's end, after trying other trainers or methodologies that simply did not work. We offer very intensive programs with guarantees for these types of situations. We guarantee to stick with you until the solution, no matter how long that takes, without charging you more money.

What inspired you to become a dog trainer?

Neil Cohen: I've always been a crazy dog person and have owned multiple dogs over the course of my life. None of our family dogs were ever formally trained, I am sure they needed it, we just didn't know how much they needed it. Honestly, we never gave much thought to dog training. Our dogs had a large yard and a dog run, so we didn't really walk them or interact with other dogs, and maybe we just accepted certain behaviors.

After growing up and moving to the suburbs with my own family, we decided to adopt Cody, he was a pretty large boxer...70 pounds of muscle. He was the best dog. He loved everyone he met, which also meant knocking people over in the process, pulling on the leash to get to them and a variety of other issues. At the time, I had a three year old who was repeatedly getting knocked over and it started to become a question of whether or not having Cody as a member of our family was sustainable. I really wanted to keep my dog. We had a very close bond, he was my hiking buddy, and I was willing to do anything to keep him in our lives. I tried it all. I searched every internet page, read every book, and watched every video. I tried method after method and he learned a whole bunch of tricks. But he continued to knock people down and pull hard on the leash, because we were not making any changes to his obedience when it came to those behaviors.

Fortunately, in my frantic internet searches, I came across the founder of Sit Means Sit, Fred Hassen. He was posting a new video everyday on YouTube, showing you everything that was possible to do with your dog. I started binge watching all of his videos, in addition to any video I could find from Sit Means Sit trainers. I was hooked. I became so enthralled that I looked into buying a franchise, but it didn't work out for me at the time because I had a business and other obligations. I continued to learn about Sit Means Sit in my free time and patiently waited for one to open near my home. When it finally happened, I became close friends with the owner who helped me tremendously with my dog. Then we started talking about me working for him part-time. Shortly after I started working for Sit Means Sit, the owner had the opportunity to move out to the West coast to run a master franchise in Los Angeles. He offered to sell me his company. And in one life-changing moment, I said "Okay". I handed off my other business to my partner, and moved to Vegas for a month to learn the Sit Means Sit methodologies and practices. I opened my business five years ago, have trained hundreds of dogs and enjoyed countless successes. I even met my wife and some of my closest friends through dog training. Everything I have today, I owe to Sit Means Sit.

How can people find out more about you, Sit Means Sit, and how you can help?

Neil Cohen: All of our programs start out with a no cost, no obligation consultation. Some of those are done over the phone. We can discuss what is going on and lay out a program that works for you and your dog. Sometimes it is more involved and there are behaviors we need to see from your dog in person. We need to see how your dog responds to us as trainers. In this case we would invite you in for the consultation. This is an opportunity for you to ask questions. How does my dog respond to this? What does your office look like? Where is my dog going to be sitting? How do you keep it clean? All of these factors are really important. It all comes down to being able to meet the needs and expectations of you and your dog, which is the foundation for success!

WEBSITE: www.sitmeanssitct.com or sitmeanssitwestchester.com

EMAIL: info@sitmeanssitct.com

OFFICE: 203-408-6599

CELL: 914-447-0567

LOCATION: Sit Means Sit Dog Training of Southern Westchester & Stamford, 4 Broadway Valhalla, NY 10595

WHAT NEIL'S CLIENTS ARE SAYING

"Neil is seriously THE BEST!!!! My dog had quite a few issues and as a new dog owner I had ZERO confidence or knowledge in handling him. I can not thank Neil and his staff enough for the help and guidance I received. I feel a thousand times more confident and know that if any issues arises I can text Neil and get help ASAP. The most important thing is my dog instantly bonded with Neil and I know hiring him was the best thing we did as a family. He still goes crazy when he sees him and showers him in kisses. Thanks Neil and staff!!!"

- Jo and dog Roscoe (Jack Russel mix), Stamford, CT

"When I rescued my dog Patches, who is a Pit Bull, Patches was abandoned in a Bronx apartment. He had problems of jumping on people, he would bark, and he was very hyper. So when I hired Neil at Sit Means Sit. He came over my house and explained his way of training. He was very impressive.and professional. So after taking patches for 3 Monday's for 8 hrs, I was amazed the difference in his behavior. He was like a different dog. He didn't jump or bark . And he was excellent at obeying commands. I would highly recommend Neil to train anybody's dog. I'm so happy with the new behavior of patches. He's like a complete different dog thanks to Neil. And of course I have to take some credit because I listened to Neil. And did reps every day."

- Rich and dog Patches (Pit Bull mix), Croton-on-Hudson, NY

"I searched far and wide for the perfect trainer for me and my service animal Charm. I could not have been luckier to have found Neil at Sit means Sit. He truly understands dogs and the way they learn and how to make them succeed. I could not be happier with the progress help and true camaraderie that Sit Means Sit offers. Thank you for helping me and Charm become the best team ever. Highly recommend to anyone who loves their dog and wants a trainer who will love them too."

- Alison and dog Charm (Cockapoo), Yonkers, NY

Curtis Day

Owner/Trainer

Sit Means Sit Casper, Wyoming

Curtis Day is the proud owner of Sit Means Sit Casper, Wyoming. He bought the location in 2018 when it went up for sale. Before becoming the owner, his two dogs trained through the same location. Previously, Curtis was a tow truck operator and manager for one of the largest companies in Casper. Traveling has never been an issue for him, so owning a large territory with hours between towns makes for a nice road trip to pick up a dog.

Curtis currently owns 4 dogs. Sindri is a Dutch Shepherd, Sieben is a Yellow lab, Derby and Ellie are both Black Labs. He has always had a passion for dogs, which is one reason he jumped on the opportunity to buy the location. He is actively seeking continuing education opportunities and believes there is always room to learn about the newest techniques and methodologies.

Credentials: AKC Evaluator, K-9 Caring Angels Therapy Dog Evaluator, Pet CPR Instructor

Tell us about your business and the types of people/dogs that you help.

Curtis Day: I am the owner of Sit Means Sit in Casper, Wyoming. We help dog owners struggling with basic obedience, aggression, socialization in puppies and adult dogs, and other behavior issues that are making it difficult to get the most out of life with their dog.

What inspired you to become a dog trainer?

Curtis Day: About nine years ago, I participated in Sit Means Sit training with two of my dogs. Throughout my life, I always had a passion for dogs. I enjoyed helping dogs and spent a lot of my free time volunteering at shelters. I was a successful manager of one of the largest towing companies in town, but I was ready for a life change. As destiny would have it, the Sit Means Sit location near my home went up for sale. I immediately jumped on the opportunity. I am proud to say that on an average day, we see about sixty dogs. We provide a variety of services including training, boarding, and daycare.

It is extremely rewarding to have the opportunity to give a dog a better life. For example, we often see dog owners at their wit's end with an aggressive dog. They are so exhausted and feel that putting the dog down is the only option. This is where we get to step in, formulate a plan, see it through, and really help the owner to be able to help their dog. It is a win-win for everyone involved. The owner develops control and learns to teach obedience so they can enjoy going out in public and having positive interactions with their dog. The dog gets a second chance at the happy life it deserves.

A great example that comes to mind is an English Mastiff that came to me with significant aggression issues. His owner had been searching all over the area for a trainer that was the right fit. His goal was to get his dog to become a therapy dog. The main issues we focused on were aggression towards other dogs and men. Fast forward to today, and he is one of our top therapy dogs. He did almost 200 hours of volunteering in the last year. This was a dog that couldn't even be taken for a walk out in public when he first came to us. Now I receive pictures of him in huge crowds and doing library events with little kids laying all over him. This is just one of the amazing transformations we get to be a part of at Sit Means Sit.

How can people find out more about you, Sit Means Sit, and how you can help?

Curtis Day: The best place to get information about Sit Means Sit Casper, Wyoming is from our Facebook page and website. The first step is a free consultation. We like to meet you and your dog in person, find out a little more about you, if you are having any specific issues, and what your goals are. We offer everything from basic obedience for family pets, to therapy dog training, to scent work training. Bringing your dog with you to this consultation is important so we can interact, give a few basic commands, and come up with a program geared specifically toward your dog.

WEBSITE: https://sitmeanssit.com/dog-training-mu/central-wyoming-dog-training/

EMAIL: sitmeanssitcapser@gmail.com

FACEBOOK:

https://www.facebook.com/SitMeansSitCentralWyoming

OFFICE: 307-251-7784

FAX: 307-337-3030

LOCATION: Sit Means Sit Dog Training of Casper, Wyoming

ADDITIONAL SERVICES: K9corraldoglodging.com

WHAT CURTIS' CLIENTS ARE SAYING

"Our dog, Mya, was a wild handful of a mess. Since her training at Sit Means Sit Casper Wy, our day to day with her is so much easier. We have since adopted another dog and Mya has just been amazing with him. Curtis and his team have been great throughout the whole thing. From the very first consultation all the way to today They have been very professional and very knowledgeable and helpful with any question or situation we have or had."

- Blake Thompson and dog Mya (German Shepherd). Casper, WY

"Sit Means Sit Casper WY has been such an incredible resource, so that I have the confidence and know-how so I can train my dog properly. Sit Means Sit has made a community where dog lovers can come together to train and learn from each other. Another great addition is the group classes offered. It is great to have a beginner class to join first, and I loved the addition of the advanced classes when we were ready to take the next step in training. Curtis and the team at Sit Means Sit have been awesome, offering so many options for training, advanced classes, and are always there with advice when I have trouble with specific skills or questions on how to improve at home."

-Julie Schmitt and dog (German Shepherd/Golden Retriever), /Casper Wy

"Sit Means Sit Casper Wy has improved the life of our dog and our relationship with her. Without Curtis and his team we were not able to help her control her aggressive/anxious behaviors.

When meeting new people, she gets overly protective and nervous. She lunges, growls, and barks at other dogs and people. She also has very high anxiety which causes her to go into her natural fight instinct in unfamiliar situations or places. Without the training from Sit Means Sit we were not able to get her attention. She is a large breed dog with a lot of strength so holding her back or getting her away was almost impossible. With the training we are able to take her places. We have the confidence that when she reacts, we will be able to get her attention even when her fight instinct is at its highest point. This gives her the opportunity to go anywhere with us instead of staying home. It keeps her safe when she puts herself in aggressive situations.

Overall, it gives her a more fulfilling life because without the Sit Means Sit we would not be able to take her anywhere with the fear that her reaction to anyone or anything might go too far and really hurt someone."

-Miranda Siebler and dog (German Shepherd), Casper, WY

Tom Longenecker

Owner/Head Trainer

Sit Means Sit Buffalo

Tom is the owner and head trainer of Sit Means Sit Dog Training located in Buffalo, New York. Tom has always had a passion for dogs and has turned that passion into a career. Tom started his training career in 2014 under Hamid Parvizian and Kris Weiss working with a husky mix he found wandering the streets of Houston, Texas. He continues to learn and work with other training experts including: Fred Hassen, Alfredo Rivera, Nino Drowaert, Bart Bellon, Lukas Miller and Chris Altherr. Tom has experience with a large assortment of breeds and temperaments. His services include helping clients get their dogs certified as therapy dogs, rehabilitating dogs with a variety of aggression issues, as well as preparing service dogs and their handlers for travel in high traffic areas such as airports and shopping malls. Tom is a registered AKC evaluator, certified remote collar expert and has competed with his dogs in Dock Diving, AKC Obedience, and PSA.

When he isn't working, Tom enjoys hiking with his dogs, playing guitar and cooking for his friends and family.

Tell us about your business and the types of people/dogs that you help.

Tom Longenecker: I have been training dogs since 2014. My main goal is to help people better enjoy their pets as members of the family. I focus on obedience for young puppies starting at eight weeks old all the way up to adult dogs. I also specialize in rehabilitation for all types of aggression including dog on dog aggression and aggression with people. A common issue I encounter is resource guarding. Resource guarding occurs when a dog is displaying behaviors such as snapping or barking to warn other dogs or humans to steer clear of the object he is "guarding". This object is often food, a favorite toy, or in some cases, a human. In addition, I help owners to overcome problems with leash reactivity. Some dogs become aggressive or feel threatened when put on a leash, and therefore act out when they see other dogs due to this insecure feeling. In my years of training, I have been very successful at helping people with these particular behaviors, as well as everything in between.

What inspired you to become a dog trainer?

Tom Longenecker: Like many people in the dog training industry, I started off as a client for another dog trainer. I owned a dog that would sometimes be aggressive with other dogs and didn't have great obedience either. She wouldn't come when called and just didn't seem to listen very well. After finding a trainer that was a good fit for me and my dog, I started to develop an interest and a passion for dog training. I was being helped tremendously and I wanted to be able to provide this same service for others. I started my career by shadowing and going through several mentorship programs. It developed into a successful dog training business that I now run on my own.

How can people find out more about you, Sit Means Sit, and how you can help?

Tom Longenecker*:* I always offer a free consultation. As I said, it's important that you are able to have a personal connection with your dog trainer because this is a familial issue. We consider dogs to be members of the family. The best way to reach me would be to contact my office. My office number is (716) 320-1565. You can also reach me at sitmeanssitbuffalo@gmail.com. We offer everything from private lessons to more intensive boarding and day camps. We can definitely find a good fit for you and your dog!

WEBSITE: https://sitmeanssit.com/dog-training-mu/buffalo-dog-training/

EMAIL: sitmeanssitbuffalo@gmail.com

OFFICE: 716-320-1565

LOCATION: Sit Means Sit Buffalo

WHAT TOM'S CLIENTS ARE SAYING

"I recently started training with Sit Means Sit for Koda. I can't express how INCREDIBLE this training has been and we've only had two sessions. She is a changed girl, soooo happy, listens and attentive to me. Sit Means Sit gets ALL the stars."

-Jess T. and dog Koda (Vizsla), Buffalo NY

"Tom trained our former street dog and worked miracles! Our dog started as highly dog reactive and could not look at another dog without losing her mind, and after her sessions with Tom, she is now in training for flyball and has her therapy dog certification. She can now stand in the flyball ring with a giant border collie running at her like a freight train and she will sit looking at me with no problem. Tom also did a fabulous job at teaching me how to work with my dog and set me up to be a successful dog handler. If you want your dog trained properly, Tom's your guy!"

-Rosie M. and dog Mama (Pit Bull), Houston TX

"Trying to convince our Yorkie that she wasn't in charge of our home was proving difficult. Bringing Tom (Sit Means Sit) into the mix has allowed us to reclaim control and put our pup on the road to good canine citizenship! Tom's easy-going manner, along with his firm straight-forward instructions, have helped transform our Yorkie into a more obedient canine, and made my wife and I better pet owners...a real "win-win!"

-Tommy P. and dog Twinkles (Yorkie), Buffalo NY

Audra Mather

Owner/Lead Trainer

Sit Means Sit

Working in all aspects of training and handling dogs since she could hold a leash, Audra developed a lifelong passion for training and behavior. This led her to a career in behavioral medicine, but her passion for dogs was always there. She continued to train her own dogs, and continued to pursue her "degree in dog" until she became well versed in a wide variety of training methods and theories. Choosing to follow her heart, Audra opened Sit Means Sit Lansing. She now uses this extensive knowledge of behavior to help find effective solutions for problems and to help you have the relationship that you want with your dog.

Tell us about your business and the types of people/dogs that you help.

Audra Mather: I consider myself a "balanced" dog trainer, which means that I do not focus too much on any one particular type of training. I am continually seeking the best fit for each dog and family. A custom training program is created based on individual needs. I specialize in aggression and reactivity issues. But that does not mean those are the only animals I help. The bread and butter of my day is working with dogs that have bad manners. Often, these are dogs that are stressing their owners out because they have absolute control over the household, making daily life extremely difficult. The end goal is to help build a positive relationship between the owner and the dog and help teach the dog appropriate behavior for living in a human household.

What inspired you to become a dog trainer?

Audra Mather: I have always been an animal lover and dreamed of becoming a veterinarian growing up. When I was 18, I got a sport bred German Shepherd. She was my first dog. I like to say I got a "Porsche" of a dog. She was crazy, protective, and defensive. I literally felt like I had a wild beast at the other end of the leash and I could barely control her. I began looking for a trainer and didn't find a single one that could help me with this dog. The only people I found were guys who did protection sports with their big German Shepherds and people who only trained with cookies, not understanding the nature of my dog at all. So I wasted a lot of time trying to solve every problem with a treat and trying to make my dog fit into a particular mold. I quickly realized that using the same formula for every dog and every issue is not sustainable. And I ended up figuring out my dog and how to handle her on my own. This is where my love for training dogs began. I loved learning about behavior and exploring new ways to solve problems.

I spent many years doing this as a nearly full time hobby. All of my free time outside of my normal work in the medical field was spent training dogs. It was then that my mother fell ill. I was forced to leave my job to take care of her at the end of her life. When it came time for me to return to my career, I didn't. I took a minimum wage job at a dog kennel to start exploring my passion from the ground up. And I never looked back. I started managing two very large boarding and daycare facilities and training dogs part time. Then I stumbled across Sit Means Sit in Madison, Wisconsin and met Mike Wheeler. He confirmed that there was no "one size fits all" training approach for dogs, which was a concept I had struggled with for years. I was introduced to a group of some of the most elite dog trainers in the world and immediately knew I had to be a part of it. After three months, I bought a franchise. The Sit Means Sit program achieves amazing results. And even better, the program is completely transferable, meaning we can teach owners to achieve the same results on their own at home with their dog. The dogs I train through Sit Means Sit are happier and more confident, which translates to happy, confident owners as well.

How can people find out more about you, Sit Means Sit, and how you can help?

Audra Mather: The first consultation is always free. This will allow you to meet the trainer, get a feel for the facility, and learn about Sit Means Sit philosophies. At this session, we will also evaluate your dog and answer any questions you might have.

WEBSITE: https://sitmeanssit.com/dog-training-mu/lansing-mi-dog-training/

EMAIL: audra@sitmeanssit.com

OFFICE: 517-225-2528

CELL: 608-713-8172

LOCATION: Sit Means Sit Lansing, MI

WHAT AUDRA'S CLIENTS ARE SAYING

"I am so thankful for Sit Means Sit and especially Audra! I have a 1-year-old German Shepherd who was uncontrollable on a leash. He hated anything that moved: people, dogs, bikes, and especially cars. It was so frustrating and stressful and I was afraid that either he or I would get hurt. We had tried 2 other training companies and I was convinced that he would never change. I decided to do the free consultation after meeting Audra at the dog fest. She said she could fix his behavior and while I was somewhat skeptical I was willing to give it a try. We did the 14-day immersion program and it was the best decision! He came back and I could tell he had learned a lot. We were able to go for walks without him pulling me and we were able to walk past distractions without a reaction. This is something I had not been able to do for months. While we still have some work to do, I know the team at sit means sit will help us along the way! Highly recommended!"

-Paige D. and dog Nitro (German Shepherd), Madison, WI

"My boyfriend and I adopted our sweet Lucy in March shortly after her 2nd Birthday. She was originally part of one of the groups of dogs brought up from an overflowing shelter in Mississippi. The couple we adopted her from rescued her from the Human Society here in Madison. After a year with Lucy they made the difficult but commendable decision to find another home from her. During that year with them Lucy was crated at least 12 hours a day due to their busy schedules and gained 23 pounds. Shortly after she entered our lives we noticed that she was very reactive to new people (especially males) and had quite a bit of anxiety. The poor girl was afraid of everything from leaves falling out of trees to us folding laundry. The longer she was with us, the happier we could tell she was becoming. Each day there was something new and exciting that she was able to discover and experience, however, her anxiety was still very much holding her back. A friend also had a dog with anxiety problems and highly recommended us to check out Sit Means Sit. We had our consultation with Audra and at first (like many others I'm sure) I was very skeptical. It's not cheap and I was not the most comfortable with the idea of using the collars. However, I loved Audra's energy and passion for what she does and she assured me that she too was skeptical when she first started. She let me check out the collar and even let me feel it on my hand, I couldn't really feel much, but totally not painful. Her confidence that she could help Lucy sold us and we signed up for the 10 Day Transformation Academy. Lucy stayed with Audra for 10 days in the beginning of June and since then we have had 4 private lessons with her and now have been going to group classes twice a week (or at least we try to!). We look forward to classes each week because it is a community of people going through everything you are and who doesn't love a room full of dogs! Now Lucy is a whole different dog. She is confident, happy, playful, and curious. Her obedience is off the charts. We knew we had a smart dog but refocusing her anxious mind into working for us has helped her tremendously and I am confident that she will only keep improving. It has only been a short 2.5 months but the progress our sweet girl has made is incredible. I will note that her sustained progress isn't just from going to the lessons and classes, if you want this for your dog there is a lot of work you must put in at home. From the time we wake up in the morning until the time we all snuggle up in bed at night to watch Netflix, Lucy is being worked. Everything we do is an opportunity to work on her obedience and refocus her anxious little mind, whether it's putting her in place while we cook or even playing fetch. If you have a dog that is struggling then I cannot recommend Sit Means Sit enough. Their knowledge, personal attention (they will answer your calls or texts with questions any time of day), and love for what they do is incredible. We are very happy with the progress Lucy has made and cannot wait to see what awesome tricks we can continue to learn in the future."

-*Sarah Elizabeth and dog Lucy (Mixed breed), Madison WI*

"Meatball, my rescue pitbull developed severe dog aggression at about 1 year old. He was a perfect angel in the house but once we were outside he turned into a devil. If he saw another dog when we were walking he would bark, scream and lunge wildly trying to get at the other dog and it took all of my strength to hold him back. Then my worst fear happened, he bit a neighbor's dog. I didn't know what to do, I didn't want to put him down, but didn't want him to hurt anyone else. I spoke with my vet and he suggested I call Audra at Sit Means Sit. He was right, the best dog trainer, ever! Meaty did a 10 day board & train program followed by some 1 on 1 lessons and now we are in group class. I can actually take him for a safe stress free walk now, no more freak on a leash. This training saved my dogs life, literally. Best investment you will make."

-Jessica and dog Meatball (Pit Bull), Lansing MI

HP Parvizian

Dog Trainer

Sit Means Sit

Originally born in Washington DC, HP's family moved to Houston, Texas where they lived throughout his high school years. After graduating, HP attended the European University in Montreux, Switzerland where he double majored in Finance and Marketing, and received a minor in Public Relations in 2004. After college, HP returned to Houston, Texas to help his father with the family business.

HP began training dogs for Sit Means Sit in 2008. He purchased the Houston, Texas location in 2010, has since expanded to 3 other locations and is preparing to launch a new pet retreat concept. HP is a leader and mentor within the Sit Means Sit Dog Training retreat franchise. HP's passion for animal care has developed into a full-time career of providing quality care for dogs and peace of mind for clients.

In 2015, HP became a board member of The Go Team Therapy Dogs. HP has seen firsthand the importance and benefit of therapy dogs in changing the lives of those they visit. HP has published and been interviewed in numerous magazines and websites for his work with animals as well as his work with therapy dogs. He also helped start the Pet of the Week program on Radio Station 104 KRBE where a new rescue dog is featured each week to help them find a new home. HP's own dogs were hired for a History Channel episode.

HP Parvizian is a certified pet first aid and CPR instructor. He conducts lessons for pet owners, pet professionals, and first responders throughout the community. HP also teaches bite prevention for the United States Postal Service, Centerpoint Energy, educational institutions, and local families. He has been featured on Channel 2 News in Houston helping with a segment on protection dogs.

HP works alongside with the following professional and community groups:

- BARC Animal Shelter & Adoption
- Supporter of the Fire & Police Departments
- Association of Professional Dog Trainers Member
- International Association of Canine Professionals member

Tell us about your business and the types of people/dogs that you help.

HP Parvizian: We serve clients from every walk of life no matter what their needs, challenges, or goals are. Our specialties include off leash training, aggression and behavior modification, and working with high energy dogs. One special area of focus is working with owners or dogs that are deaf. We are able to help them develop communication skills and foster relationships even with disabilities that would typically make this difficult. We pride ourselves on recognizing and appreciating the unique needs of each dog and dog owner. Dogs don't need to be "bad" in order to benefit from training. I like to say "We make bad dogs good and good dogs great."

I continually tell my clients not to think of our services in terms of "obedience" training. Obedience implies that I tell you what to do and you do it. We want to look at dog training in terms of "behavior". A behavior is an action that we are going to perform without having to think about it, such as driving a car or washing our hands. We don't have to think about the process or be reminded how. The goal is to create new behaviors for our dogs and to expect 1% improvement each time. I use the 1% rule with my clients quite often. Each time we do something, I want the dog to be 1% better...1% quieter, 1% faster in "coming" to me, 1% less pulling on the leash. It will never be perfect in the beginning. The dog will still bark or pull on that leash. This provides us the opportunity to continue to reinforce the behaviors we want.

Over time, the behavior exponentially becomes better and better. We get to enjoy the time with our dogs that much more. It translates to happy dogs AND happy owners. This is the perfect cycle for building communication and relationships with our companion animals.

What inspired you to become a dog trainer?

HP Parvizian: Growing up, my family was in the Oriental rug business and a dog can be public enemy number one for rugs. I never thought to ask for a dog because dogs simply were not allowed in my home. But I thoroughly enjoyed playing with everyone else's dogs. I got my first dog when I went off to college and became hooked on everything canine. We spent a lot of time together. I loved watching training videos. I enjoyed apprenticing with other trainers and gathering as much information as I could. About 12 years ago I was at a pivotal point in my life where I left corporate America to enter the world of professional dog training.

I wanted to follow my passion. I jumped in head first and fell in love with this new career. It is extremely rewarding to see the positive changes I can bring to people's lives. Dogs that came to me aggressive are now therapy dogs, making their owners proud and bringing joy to others . Owners that were once stressed out over a hyperactive puppy are able to enjoy life with their dog after training. I honestly feel like I haven't worked a day in 12 years because I enjoy what I do and feel good about the results we achieve.

How can people find out more about you, Sit Means Sit, and how you can help?

HP Parvizian: Just by mentioning this book, you will receive a free gift and a special training offer. The best way to contact us is via our website at sitmeanssithouston.com. You can set up a free consultation, meet with me or another member of our talented training team and learn more about our programs geared to meet the individual needs of you and your dog.

WEBSITE: sitmeanssithouston.com

EMAIL: office@sitmeanssithouston.com

OFFICE: 281-912-3647

LOCATION: Sit Means Sit Dog Training - Houston & Katy

WHAT HP'S CLIENTS ARE SAYING

"We love SMS Houston. We were struggling with behavior issues with our Shiloh Shepherd puppy and were bringing twin babies into the house in addition to already having a seven year old. We needed to get the puppy under control. We tried puppy school at a big box and it was a complete waste of time and money as it did not work at all.

After doing some research, we made the decision to call SMS Houston and get a free evaluation. HP came out to our Home and evaluated Fergie. He briefly worked with her and by the end of the 45 minute evaluation she was staying in place which she had never done before. We were sold!

We sent her to SMS and HP did her immersion training for 11 days. We joke that we got a different dog back. Having a 90lb puppy that was bad mannered was not something that could continue. She went from being super hyper on a leash to being successfully walked by our seven year old. She comes and sit/stays on command and we got the added bonus of her being fully crate trained when we got her back as she would howl previously prior to her training.

We are taking full advantage of the lifetime group classes and are continuing to reinforce her training. HP has made two follow up house calls to make sure that we were doing okay and to make sure that she was not regressing to prior bad behaviors. (She hasn't)

I would highly recommend having your dog trained by SMS Houston. HP and his team are miracle workers and have so much passion for your pet and their training. It is worth every cent. It is an awesome feeling to be able to take your dog out anywhere including high distraction places and have a non-reactive dog. Calling SMS will be the best decision you could make for your pet and having them properly trained."

-Jennifer B. and dog Shiloh (Shepherd), Houston, Tx

"Sit means sit changed our lives. I couldn't take my dog anywhere without her misbehaving or attacking other dogs. Now I can take her anywhere, she's got perfect manners no matter what. My family's quality of life has improved greatly and I'm so proud of my dog. HP, Kritter, and ALL of the dog trainers there are top notch, fabulous dog trainers. I can contact them anytime if I have a question outside of my training sessions. There's no one else I trust with my dog more than the Sit Means Sit Team.

There's no question about who's the best dog trainer in Houston, it's Sit Means Sit hands down."

-Emily S. and dog Lucy (German Shepherd), Houston TX

"Dear reader,

Let me tell you the long story about my dog Kimmy the German Shepherd. Go back in time to September 2016. Exactly the 25th I received a call from a friend asking for help to rescue this dog that was dumped at a construction site. As an animal lover that I am, I went with my daughter and after 2 hours of coercing, chicken nuggets, hamburgers (I do watch hope for paws rescues) we finally rescued her. 42 lbs at the vet , emaciated, and full of worms, Kimmy began her new life at my house. I have had mostly rescued dogs all my life so I thought I was an avid dog owner and nothing would ever happen. Was I wrong, Kimmy started to show reactions towards people and dogs when walking or when people were coming to the house.

On one of our constant trips to the vet (she had stomach bleeding issues her first year with us), one of the vet techs recommends Sit Means Sit, a place that for sure would reject her as she was you could say "wild from being so terrified'.To our surprise, they accept her and here comes chapter 2 of her life. As months go by, and with the help of HP telling me what I was doing wrong, how I was confusing the dog, and how I was the one not following directions, things started to look great until August 25, 2017. Before I forget, Kimmy was certified as a good canine companion in April of 2017.

Chapter 3, my family gets flooded during Harvey, and we ended up being rescued by boat to being dumped at a place full of scared humans and animals, to again being dumped in the middle of a freeway for another 2 hours to end up by a miracle from God rescued by a hotel van. For the next month, between cleaning the flooded house, and trying to find a place to live at, Kimmy had to endure the back and forth, the feelings of destruction, the feelings of what we do, and she really was a champion, being very good. Finally, we found a place and after 2 weeks Kimmy decided to start trying to taste ankles; again I called HP for help, immediately he comes over and teaches me what to do and reminds me of all those trainings we have participated at. So, slowly, but sure things start to get better, not perfect, but better.

Chapter 4, HP and Sit Means Sit goes into transitioning places, trainings are done at different locations, and Kimmy seems fine with all this; in fact she likes the distractions as she gets praised more often to act as she is expected.

Chapter 5, today May 17, 2018, right after coming back from training nice and hot, I proceeded to do something I have done so many times, to let her go to sit at the metal gated fence to wait for me to be opened, and what does she do, she saw something and got her head stuck in the fence with no way for me to help her out. Again I called HP for help and after a long time (whole ordeal lasted around 2 hours) HP and my son finally got her out. For what it seems like a not big deal, the dog did panic at the beginning and I just went into full training mood, having her focus on me and follow my directions, I was you could say calm on the outside, and firm too with her reassuring that help was on the way and we were going to get out, and we did!

So, what Sit Means Sit Houston has done for me and my family? They have taught us We are the ones that need to be corrected for the dog to be successful; We are the ones that need to dedicate time on a daily basis to keep on training the dog; We are the ones at fault when our dog makes mistakes, they just follow our body language; We are the ones that let our dogs do whatever they want, We are the ones that help the dog gain confidence and trust, We are the ones that will help the dogs in emergency situations and We are the ones that absolutely adore our dogs.

So, If you want to have a companion for life that goes with you to restaurants, stores, bars, behaves wonderful and loves you to death, then Sit Means Sit- Houston is for you, but if you want a dog that acts like a robot with no personality, then it will be better to find another place. I am forever thankful to HP and Sit Means Sit to be with me when I have needed him; reactive, flood, bites and head stuck in a metal fence. Thanks with all my heart, and if any of you want to meet me and Kimmy, just let me know."

-Susy Brown and dog Kimmy (German Shepherd) Houston, TX

Lisa York

Dog Trainer

Sit Means Sit

I can't recall a time in my life when I didn't have a dog or wasn't training a dog. My first dog, Stormy, a Doberman, was the center of my sixth-grade world. I competed with him in AKC Obedience and he won many titles. I loved every aspect of training!

As a "grown up", I joined the business world in the HR/staffing field, and ultimately became the CEO of a staffing firm. I considered myself successful, and I really enjoyed helping people with their career objectives, but along the way, I spent all my free time training my German Shepherds and I dreamed of being able to make a living training dogs and helping people to more fully enjoy their relationship with their dogs.

I have spent countless hours training in the IGP sport (Schutzhund/IPO), starting out my days at 6:00 a.m. to go tracking with my dogs. I have titled several German Shepherds (BH, Tracking and Obedience). My dogs absolutely love the sport! Training through play, but also having rules that the pack lives by, makes my dogs happy and eager to train.

I found Sit Means Sit when I had a German Shepherd that showed signs of aggression, something I had not experienced before with my sport dogs. I was baffled by her behavior and tried everything I knew to fix it. Sit Means Sit was the only place I found that was fully willing and able to work through the behavior.

I learned so much from the trainers on how to recognize the emotional side of the fear that my dog was feeling, and how to show leadership to ease the fear, thus allowing the training to work. This was a huge thing for me to learn, even after so many years of training. The trainers worked through the specific issues and gave me new tools that really made a difference for me and my dog.

I knew I needed to be a part of the Sit Means Sit family because I wanted to help people have happy, confident, and obedient dogs. The opportunity to purchase Sit Means Sit San Antonio came along at the perfect time, so now I have the job of my dreams!

Tell us about your business and the types of people/dogs that you help.

Lisa York: Our locations include Sit Means Sit San Antonio and Sit Means Sit New Braunfels, which is a suburb of San Antonio. We work with many different kinds of dogs. Most often, people come to us for behavioral issues with their dog such as aggression. For example, we see many people who have a difficult time walking their dog because it is reactive to other dogs and they are looking for a way to manage this behavior.

In addition to behavior training, we provide baseline training for service and therapy dogs if people are interested in getting their dogs into that arena. The main focus of this type of training is excellent obedience under extreme distraction. It takes a skilled trainer to get a service dog into the mental space between thought and deed.

We like to say that we "train as you live." We want the owner to be able to go places with their dog, have a dog that walks nicely on a leash, and have a dog that behaves well when the doorbell rings. The end goal is a functional, fun dog that you can enjoy as a member of your family.

What inspired you to become a dog trainer?

Lisa York: It all began back in sixth grade when I got a Doberman Pinscher for Christmas. This dog became my everything. He was my world and the sun, moon and stars revolved around this dog. Prior to receiving him, I had to write a long essay to my father detailing all of the things I would do to take care of my own dog. I wrote five pages including everything from feeding to training, to prove I deserved this dog that I had been begging for. I began taking him to a local roller skating rink where they held dog training lessons every Wednesday night. I did this with him for two years as I watched him evolve into this wonderful dog and companion.

We then started AKC sport work where he won quite a few titles and was expanding his repertoire of tricks including opening the refrigerator and putting garbage in the trash can. My parents were very impressed and told me that "I really had a knack for this", encouraging me to go into dog training as a profession. At the time, I felt that it would not serve me financially and I became CEO of a staffing company, still continuing to do sport work on the side. I was doing a particular sport work with my German Shepherds called Schutzhund, which is a protection sport in Germany. It became my obsession. Literally, it was all I could think about. I knew I had to find a way to make this my profession and decided it was never too late to live out your dream. I was having great success training my own dogs and began helping others as well. I entered the Sit Means Sit system and never looked back.

How can people find out more about you, Sit Means Sit, and how you can help?

Lisa York*:* We offer free consultations to all of our clients. You can choose an over the phone or in person consultation. In person, we will sit down with you and your dog for about an hour. We will watch the behavior of your dog, talk with you, show you examples of other dogs that we train and give you a tour of our 6,0000 square foot facility. This will provide you with a glimpse into a day in the life of a dog that receives training through us. If you feel more comfortable over the phone, we will be happy to send you videos of dogs that we train, as well as a video tour of the facility. We have special military discounts and other discounted programs that we can share with you.

WEBSITE: www.sitmeanssitsatx.com

EMAIL: lisa@sitmeanssitsatx.com

OFFICE: 210-414-2788

LOCATION: Sit Means Sit San Antonio, TX

WHAT LISA'S CLIENTS ARE SAYING

"I sought out Sit Means Sit to help with dog reactivity, which began very early for Henrik after he had a bad experience with an adult dog and a medical condition that limited early socialization. This defensive reactivity impacted his life (and our lives) in a big way. Even neighborhood walks were a nightmare, as he'd begin barking and lunging at dogs half a block away. We tried other programs, but saw no improvement. We came to SMS when he was 11 months old, and it's been a game changer. He's learned to focus on me rather than other dogs, and his confidence has increased so much. We now can go for walks and have no problems meeting or passing other dogs. I regularly take him with me to dog friendly places around town. He even has dog friends that he's excited to see and play with at group class. He still has a tendency toward reactivity, but I now know how to set him up to succeed and what to do if we get into a situation where he's triggered. A highpoint of this past year was when he earned his CGC, CGCU and CGCA. I hope to eventually do therapy work with him."

-Deb E. and dog Henrik (GSD), San Antonio, TX

"Bear is a typical energetic puppy, and we felt like we were able to teach him some basic obedience, but consistently struggled to have guests over to our house or to take Bear anywhere due to his energy and need for attention. The main behavioral struggles we wanted to address were impulse control, pulling when walking, jumping when greeting people, destructive chewing, and not coming when called. We have seen vast improvements in all those areas since training with Sit Means Sit, as well as an all-around improved attentiveness and obedience to us and our commands. A great recent example of his improved behavior was when he remained on 'place' throughout Christmas morning and all the associated excitement! Bear continues to surprise our friends and family as they often say...It's like night and day!"

-Brian W. and dog Bear (Goldendoodle), San Antonio, TX

"I first found out about Sit Means Sit from a friend who explained that she went through a training program that worked very well in her favor. We started our Day Camp Training Program towards the end of December 2019. I instantly loved the way all the trainers accepted and loved Cookie and her "scary" bark and didn't even bat an eye, like some places do, when they see a pit bull. I have had people judge my dog before, and SMS did not do that. Instead, they are always there to help me work on things and genuinely want what's best for me and my dog. After the first 2 weeks, we saw an amazing improvement. Cookie, 5 years old, had some manners, but we wanted to work on her protective behaviors. She responds so much better to my commands. I especially love the group classes designed for reactive dogs. We have only been to 5 group classes and she no longer chases cats, barks at other dogs, or tries to scare off things that get too close. I am so proud and happy we chose Sit Means Sit."

-Angela Q. and dog Cookie (Pit Bull), San Antonio, TX

ABOUT THE PUBLISHER

Mark Imperial is a Best-Selling Author, Syndicated Business Columnist, Syndicated Radio Host, and internationally recognized Stage, Screen, and Radio Host of numerous business shows spotlighting leading experts, entrepreneurs, and business celebrities.

His passion is discovering noteworthy business owners, professionals, experts, and leaders who do great work, and sharing their stories and secrets to their success with the world on his syndicated radio program titled "Remarkable Radio".

Mark is also the media marketing strategist and voice for some of the world's most famous brands. You can hear his voice over the airwaves weekly on Chicago radio and worldwide on iHeart Radio.

Mark is a Karate black belt, teaches kickboxing, loves Thai food, House Music, and his favorite TV shows are infomercials.

Learn more:
www.MarkImperial.com
www.ImperialAction.com
www.RemarkableRadioShow.com